SHIPBREAKING

SHIPBREAKING

Robin Beth Schaer

2014 Robert Dana-Anhinga Prize for Poetry

Selected by Jan Beatty

Anhinga Press
Tallahassee, Florida 2015

Cover art: Leslie Baum, "Mementos, C.B.," 2014, oil on sintra
             Courtesy of the artist. www.lesliebaum.net
Cover design, book design, and production: Carol Lynne Knight
Type Styles: text set in Adobe Jensen Light and titles set in Futura

Library of Congress Cataloging-in-Publication Data
Shipbreaking by Robin Beth Schaer, First Edition
ISBN – 978-1-934695-44-9
Library of Congress Cataloging Card Number – 2015936966

Anhinga Press Inc. is dedicated wholly to the
publication and appreciation of fine poetry and other literary genres.

For personal orders, catalogs and information write to:
Anhinga Press
P.O. Box 3665
Tallahassee, Florida 32315
Website: www.anhingapress.org
Email: info@anhinga.org

Published in the United States
by Anhinga Press
Tallahassee, Florida
First Edition, 2015

For my parents

CONTENTS

THREE

ACKNOWLEDGMENTS

Thank you to the editors of the following publications, in which these poems originally appeared:

At Length: "Natural History"
The Awl: "Fathom," "Flight Distance," "Tornado," and "Wildfire"
Barrow Street: "Safekeeping"
Denver Quarterly: "Reptilian" and "Migration"
Drunken Boat: "At Sea," "At Home," "Swarm," and "Nocturnal"
Everyday Genius: "Breakfast"
Greensboro Review: "The Liger"
Guernica: "Messenger" and "Insomnia"
The Literary Review: "Wreck" and "Coal"
Opium: "Aphelion"
Painted Bride Quarterly: "Contrition" and "Restraint"
Prairie Schooner: "Avian"
Slice: "Disturbance"
Southeast Review: "White Matter"
Spinning Jenny: "Volcano"
Tin House: "Fear" and "Yellowjackets"
Tuesday; An Art Project: "Little Ice Age"
Washington Square: "Iceland"

Best New Poets (University of Virginia Press): "The Liger"
Starting Today: 100 Poems for Obama's First 100 Days (University of Iowa Press): "Endangerment Finding"

The completion of these poems was greatly aided by fellowships from Yaddo, Djerassi Resident Artists Program, Virginia Center for the Creative Arts, and Saltonstall Foundation for the Arts.

Deep love to Anthony and Faro for being my beacons and guiding me home through uncertainties, mysteries, and doubts. Endless gratitude to my parents and brothers for keeping me afloat for so long. A standing ovation to Leslie Baum for her stunning artwork. Big thanks to Jan Beatty, Lynne, Kristine, Jay, Jessica, and all the lovely folks of Anhinga Press. A small debt to Adam. Adoration, abrazos, and rowdy toasts for my dear friends, family, teachers, and crewmates, especially Tracy and Tina for so much Magick, Lucie, Mark, Doug, Billy, Liam, Timothy, Joel, Paul, Monica, Brenda, Cathy, Meghan, Matthea, Craig, Maureen, Cate, Todd, Minnie, Beth, Elizabeth, Kristen, Elyssa, Amy, Oona, Lizzie, Kazim, Gabe, Shana, Ali, Shelly, Dana, Scotty, Chips, Marcia, Captain Robin Walbridge, and the Bounty.

SHIPBREAKING

⇥ ONE ⇤

WRECK

Hammered by stars, the island bides
its solitude with sharp trees of parakeets,

prospect fires, and years of wind.
Even coral must dream of cobwebs.

Every breath powdered down,
a legion of waves forbids my face.

This shoaled world is a hoarse hum
of shells. A refuge in halves: I am

forgiven by water, but savaged by sky.
Beyond the trooped reef, the world

is vague as horizon. My jaw is a distant
animal, the copper envy of tusks.

To return would burn the sails and rout
the heart. The sea is the opposite of falling.

MESSENGER

No one else heard the knocking; not a water drip
or transformer hum, but a distant ping pong
volley overhead. This too was in my mind

like the glass ship marooned in the forest.
When I listened closely, my elbows ached and teeth
chattered from the racket; when I drowned

the noise, trampoline springs and night owls
also faded. I tried to cure myself with mirrors
and cotton balls, but forgot arithmetic and how

to fold my shirts. All I could do was rattle.
Even in sleep I heard the din and roamed
through crowds of redwoods. Someone above

was calling. The choice left was to be lost.
I climbed cloud-high to answer. In the canopy,
the air was cold, but streets were the same

as below: wheat-paste posters peeling off walls,
and drifts of newspapers and boxes tied
with bakery twine. No antennas or banging drums,

but knocking everywhere. People appeared
swiftly around me. They rose from the branches,
silver-eyed and unbuttoned, twinned underneath.

Their sap sticky fingers covered me, searching
my pockets for coins. *What use is money in the trees?*
Their faces turned downward, toward the town

exposed like an X-ray from above: a starving dog,
a misaligned fence, the children swimming naked.
To be remembered on the ground, they answered:

a gray sentence spoken over a green one.
The chorus of their breath shook pinecones free.
With my hands held out: *I will carry your messages down.*

APHELION

Leave your country and all its weather
behind; forget the sun, the tent of sky,

the wind in vast cotillions. Choose me
instead, in this dim place under a shelter

of speculation and tin. Here we speak
the argot of twins and I know there are

creatures only you see and answers
I am not ashamed of. Cast beyond

the planets, even Pluto has a moon.
They spin with locked tides, always

faced together, married to darkness;
so stay, my consort, my lovely undoing.

DISTURBANCE

For Anthony

Put a silver coin on your tongue
with a penny underneath
and you can taste the electricity.

We said *go slow* but were urgent
as elephants, charging down
the power lines. Now the lights

won't stay on and the trees
are down. Sleep until you're done,
I'm awake, brushing hands along

darkened walls, feeling for the switch.
It must be here somewhere. We are
electric; this is not a metaphor.

Each of our cells a tiny battery:
membrane the cardboard, ions
the coins. Once, I tumbled down

a flight of stairs, then fainted
each time I tried to stand.
Overcome by nerves in riot,

the body powers down, crumples
rather than abide. Even swooning
is a kind of fainting, overwhelmed

by bliss, instead of pain. We cross
our breaking capacity: too much
current in the wires and a strip

of metal melts in sublimation.
But without the blown fuse or insulated
mica, the charge could stop a heart.

Fifteen hundred people crowded
Coney Island to watch Edison
electrocute an elephant with sixty

thousand volts. No one cared
if the men she killed fed her
lit cigarettes or if the current

was alternating. They came for spectacle,
the split desire for frenzy and obedience,
to watch a beast condemned

for being wild. Are you awake now?
There is a storm coming. Count
the distance with me. With steeples tipped

in copper, earthing rods on roofs,
we can leave the water, crouch in a field,
but we still draw lightning between us.

In the Southern Ocean, the sailors
watched balls of fire in the sails,
the luminous energy that gathers

on ships after a squall. On the shores
of Lake Superior, lightning leaves
fulgurite behind, sand fused

into rods of glass, jagged shells
holding the shape of being struck.
The rock is *amorphous*, a word I want

to believe means love without form.
It may not take the shape we expect,
but a stunning singularity instead, forked

and branched underground, impossible
to measure without breaking. But with rulers
and shovels, we approach anyway;

the sublime is a failure of the mind,
said Kant, to understand what seems
formless and boundless. Now, you hold

my face in your hands, even as lamps
flicker and dim. Maybe there is no switch.
Help me search. If we stand on wax,

clutching wire and vials, the sparks
as our lips near can be counted.
But without the mind, these motions

are only reflex. Galvani strung frogs,
severed at the spinal cord, on wire
across his rooftop and waited for lightning.

Their legs leaped and twitched, without
longing or direction, obeying the storm.
My love, I would thread your torn nerves

together, become electrogenic,
with anodes and cathodes for fingers
to soothe this arrhythmia. Suspend me

in silks and my face will glow. Current
is the cure for both a stopped heart
and one that beats too much.

And if it must be shocked twice,
the surgeons call it a *reluctant heart*.
Love is haywire. Hold fast,

between us, pass *subtle particles*
that singe and seize. We are electric.

RESTRAINT

There were no solid walls
or impossible locks. I was the Queen

of Birds, with a metal shim
beneath my tongue and a shoulder

slipped from the socket. My escape
was always astounding; the art

was finding the slack. Then you,
my sweet locomotive, careened.

Your impact shook loose sequins
and concealed keys, released a sack

of pigeons. I was not in search
of whiplash, but in your long arms,

I craved capture, the stillness
of a swaddle and would reeve myself

to you with piano wire, twine,
and rope, unrigged. I offer my wrists,

my thumbs, but the unfettering
you feel is just my finest trick.

FLIGHT DISTANCE

Sugar was grit all through my feral year.
The sleepless alarm of instinct strung
every nerve on a trigger of quills.

In this wildness, you took me clothed,
only a rattle of buckle for warning.
Not ardor, but hunger compelled

that first time. And now, after
losing count, we still uncover ourselves
last. Clothing pushed up or pulled

down, a neckline stretched across hips,
a skirt raised over head, until breathless
and bare, we smolder against skin.

Maybe this rush evades a snare, or is seized
with skittish need, but whatever spins
this frenzy does not conceal our fragile bones.

Dear rogue, keep me indoors awhile more.
When you ask me to say your name, I will.

COAL

Murmurs of brittle affairs plow
the margins with dynamite through

tender guard. In the shallows, men
pound their own eyes. Desire leaves

a slurry on the wives they go back to.
Some believe the night's language crows

in lies. But morning is a forebent darling,
misborn to obey nonsense. We goad

the backwoods with rum and toothpicks,
hours fidgeting in the undergrowth,

while wolves, those dear crooks, thieve
mildewed wheat and wool. With soliloquies

of prospect, we dive a dozen feet of chain.
It is a saint's task to prune the mountain.

BREAKFAST

You are the sort of man who takes his toast
well done. The slices fan open, each pale

velvet center is yours alone. It is better
not to think of other hands already here:

the fingers that kneaded dough, and palms
that held the loaves. Besides, the heroes

of epics always set off from ugly towns.
Your mornings start the same: coffee

percolates, eggs simmer in their pan,
a newspaper unfolds itself. The toaster

accepts the bread by design, two slices
slide in and stiffen against radiant springs;

a single purpose finds doubtless clarity.
You can sense the switch nearing its end

and hold your hands over the chrome mouth,
keeping the bread down to the edge

of burn. There is no perfection greater
than breakfast. Even the executioner

gets a baguette, though the baker sells it
upside down. The rest of the day, you follow

shadows of hawks across a field.
Your hem unravels, baby spiders hatch

in the mailbox, and the squirrel skull
on the sidewalk is only a peach pit.

But no one gets to take the zebra home,
you tell yourself, even less than a horse

would be lucky. At night, you see only
my eyes, a pair of dark fish watching you.

My hand on your thigh is flat;
you wish it could be a hot coil.

(I know all this.) In the morning,
you wake in a fist. You want to tell me

everything. Your mouth opens like a box top,
then closes with one cardboard flap tucked

into another, resealable but not airtight.
The future clock of disappointment chimes.

There is no safe word because no one
is there to hear. But breakfast will be perfect.

YELLOWJACKETS

A breach beneath the leaves, spreading cells
fill a hollow, swelling where droves

of rabbits once slept. Accidental incursion
is mine: a rake across the vespiary mouth.

The first sting is fragrant with war. Our skin
incites a thousand alarms, furious to find us.

In retreat, we scatter tools and wild ginger,
clutch our punctured arms. The killing frost

is not far, you say, debating our response.
We take sides. I tell you, the queen

will survive: overwinter, wake in spring,
build a new home, birth a new colony.

Farther south, a nest fills a Chevy
stalled out in a barn. The experts come.

There must be several queens, they decide,
with armies of workers keeping domains apart.

A strongman once found hiving bees
inside a carcass, enough to fill his hands

with honey for wedding gifts, but this ground
is not a lion's body, there is no sweetness here.

To become foundress, the queen must be
unseated. New reigns begin with massacre.

At dusk, for three nights, I empty cans
of poison into the rift. Chrysanthemum

paralysis sealed with a stone. A small intrusion
opens fractures, papers enemies. I have learned

this sibilant secret: home requires vigilance
as someone macerates, waiting to overthrow.

AT SEA

Outbound in ballast, heavy
with gravel that smells of home.

Our quarry emptied out
in another hemisphere's bay.

I saved a stone from the hold,
the shape your elbow makes

in my palm. Thirteen weeks
without anchor, only canvas

and straining rope; twice,
I breathed the solace of pines

in wind, carried off an unseen
coast. Our constellations slip

under the horizon as we sail
beyond God. My skin will never

be smooth again. Two men
already are lost, one swept

over by following seas, the other
slipped from the mast. Below

the Tropic, ghost ships
and tinsel sky are real, but a grave

beside you would be a fable.
Here, the Horn is lord, with ice

and swells high as the crosstrees.
For passage, we promise apples,

penguin hides, even our thumbs;
given now, or taken eastward.

Both crosses can never be calm.
The Pacific will bring us ashore,

to walk unswerved for more
than a yard, and a holyday

of turnips carved into flowers,
plum duff, and wooden hymns:

a charade that only deepens
the absence it bends to hide.

I would rather pray for sleep
and enough wheat to come home.

AT HOME

The copper carries my wishes.
A storm snapped a dozen trees

the day you left; the same
straight firs cut for masts.

The *Gazette* held no word,
no sight of your sails. Each week,

my fingers traced columns of ships —
Flying Cloud, Lion of Waves,

Golden Empire — with titles
broader than their beams,

bold as thoroughbreds, as if
a name could seal a fortune.

My mind slipped to the ocean
floor, littered with wrecks.

I placed silver coins
beside your picture and knit

scarves until we received
the rattle and whalebone

swallows. I send you handshakes
in return. Our son was born

this winter: eight pounds
and eager thirst, no fever.

It was three days of labor
with compress of nettle

and yarrow leaf, every knot
in the house untied. His ears

are tiny shells, hands in fists,
your brown hair. The cradle

is drawn with yellow dories.
For your birthday, a party

without you here: spongecake
and cherryade. Hope you were

given bread and molasses.
My love, remember, the polestar

is not alone, but twinned,
a pair of suns, guiding you North.

⇥ TWO ⇤

FATHOM

The dogs understand your heart
and know something of the taste

of salt. We live off incense and coins,
herding coveys of waves, wrenching

down the blues. I begged and pouted
all this cotton, but what use

is stooping to nothing. The sea
refused twenty corroded decades

before ours. Sometimes, the nets
raise a god in a flash of minnows.

Sometimes, matted ferns claim you,
their breath a weapon paused at the eye.

Always, we are capsized by the impossible
child in a thicket of empty books.

SAFEKEEPING

Run-off heavy and black as your hair,
the river rolls moraine in rapids strong
enough to sweep away a horse. I believed

a handful of you would protect me
from the whole of you, the way an eye
of blue glass will ward off the blue-eyed

desert *djinn*, or claws and jawbones will spare
the holder from being mauled. With you,
there is no safety in possession, no talisman

for your voice. The skin behind your small ears,
the anise still under my nails, only leaves me
longing entirely. Of course I was warned,

there were posts and placards, but I want
Pleistocene, to be cold, to wade within
the broken glacier, follow its melting retreat

coursed back to sea. When the ice is gone,
the bedrock will swell upward, released,
only the warm weight of moss on its back.

With fingers in the rush, a fist of ice age,
quick as ankles brushing under the table,
but enough to know, I would not fight this.

THE LIGER

Already it never happened — not the fire,
not the lion. Even the tiger fled,

leaving behind the cub too strange
to be her own, the milk teeth still loose

in his jaw. With chuff and muddled stripes,
a modest mane, he is two cats at once,

a fallow giant, both spans combined.
Not the halfling mule bred for work

or peaches grafted to plums, but a spark formed
in a great loneliness. And soon, he will be gone;

impossible lives are always short, too brief
to name. Only the farmers will remember him,

the apparition that stalked their fields. They offered
mangoes and buffalo, kept the orphan as myth.

WHITE MATTER

To begin, mistaken. The child answers
unarmed, hands up. In the margins,
the man sees a demon. The eye

is unremarkable; its weight in salt
is testimony. Yet, how small a weapon
the iris that dilates normal light.

The day is clothed in pockets. Inside
a shallow trap of noise, the child
runs as the man fires. People

watch from cars, surfaces are glass,
contusions stipple with soot. Where
is the pledge to police the heart?

Without grief, the gun is artifact;
exit wounds are conversations the bullet
denies. Anything shot into will stop.

MIDDLE FLIGHT

The baby's feet never touch the ground.
Before now, he floated in dark water
so I hold him like an exile for months

until his own weight is no longer foreign.
Someday he too will chase his lost lightness
half-remembered toward the sky. History

is full of flightless falls: metal wings
and bird machines built without destination,
just to be loose of the anchor. No one

flew until a papermaker watched
his wife's chemise swell beside a fire
and conjured a craft to ride the heat.

Like *putting a cloud in a paper bag*, he filled
the first balloon with air from burning straw
and wet wool, and launched a rooster

above Versailles. The night my son takes
his first steps, I let paper lanterns go
in the dark and watch them soar from sight.

They rise moonward, like the aeronaut
who vanished over Lake Michigan
in a muslin balloon. The sky utters reasons,

lies told to other lives. Maybe the lanterns
sink in the distance, maybe the man drowned.
Neither return home. In Brazil, a priest

hitched himself to a thousand balloons
and was gone. He must have whispered *céu*
as he climbed aloft (only in English are heaven

and sky different words). As a child, I tied
balloons to my arms and tried to rise off
the grass. I wished for distance to turn the town

miniature, into a train set with matchstick
trees and voices too far to hear. I believed
the sky was actual blue, not the elastic

scatter of light that only makes it seem so.
I still cannot hold this truth in my mind:
navy, midnight, and royal are just semblance

of elsewhere. How bitter to sacrifice wonder
for proof. Napoleon kept a balloonist
in court who was more at home above

than below. She was ugly on the ground,
startled by dogs and carriages, but daring in air,
an acrobat with fire and ostrich feathers,

until she fell from a blazing balloon, dying
that seemed like flying. Maybe there is no refuge
in suspension, no swerve from gravity

and broken cobblestone. But to hide in faith
is easier than to contend with doubt.
What moved through sky I once believed

was holy. I buried moths and blue jays, and kept
a shoe box reliquary of feathers, rockets,
and airplane spoons. Somewhere in childhood

an equation is fused between elevation
and milk. It begins this way: too tired to stand,
we reach toward arms and find altitude.

Later, we scramble up trees, climb mountains,
and sail toward the poles to be light again
with the world underneath. In California,

a truck driver strapped weather balloons
on his lawn chair to hover above his wife
and house with a sandwich and cooler of beer,

but barreled three miles up, into the path
of landing planes. A secretary in North Carolina
carried her seat to a field, floated all morning

under a cluster of balloons, then rolled it back
to her desk and finished typing a letter. Sometimes
the world is too heavy, or we are too heavy in it.

At seven, I stood under an empty sky
hoping to be taken up by a beam of light,
a tornado, or the claws of a winged beast.

I traced satellites across the dark, awake
all night in the backyard. Their orbits grew smaller
and closer with every rotation. I waited all summer

for the space station to come down and was afraid
of what else might fall. In school, the siren rang
and grammar stopped. Behind the cubbies, I knelt

before mittens, hats, and paper bags.
I pictured bombs dropping, a cloud mushrooming
over the soccer field. The sky is always strategy

for war. Decades before, beneath a silver balloon
at dawn, an Air Force colonel floated up
nineteen miles. More alone and farther than

anyone had been, he was high enough to see
the planet curve away. He radioed a message
then parachuted down: *The sky above is void,*

very black and very hostile. He was not
the first in the stratosphere, nor was an ape
or airship either. Before him, a shell lobbed

at France vaulted the height then crashed
through a cathedral roof, killing worshippers
knelt in prayer. The fallout shelters are gone now.

In my son's school, they practice clearing halls
and locking doors. They hide silent on the floor.
I no longer worry about missiles but who

has a gun instead. I thought courage was leaping
from the basket. I thought the risk was descent,
not departure. When my son loses his grip,

a yellow balloon escapes and I remember
that skyward longing, to be untethered
from my life. After drifting over Paris,

the first balloonist declared, *I felt we were*
flying away from the earth and all its troubles.
Then he left his copilot behind and rose alone

ten thousand feet. He heard his breath
and rippling silk, and watched the sun set
a second time that day. *Never has a man*

felt so solitary, so terrified, he said
and refused to fly again. When my son says,
Lift me up, I raise him over my head,

not to catch the balloon or be airborne,
but to look down on me here. Above is empty,
but earth is home, even the bombs know that.

REPTILIAN

Take this crime: I carried the alligator
home through red mangroves, in my arms. His gnarled head
cool against my neck, and his tail around me
brushing my ankles.

Brought inside the village, he shivered, needing
swamp not land. My body would never keep him
warm enough. I offered him strips of birch bark,
rabbits and quail eggs —

anything. I knew it was wrong to bring him
here; he could devour you, the children, clawing
flesh and cotton, swinging his heavy tail hard,
breaking to pieces

doors and chairs. So drown me in shallow water,
hold me under, finish this need for pebbled
hide, and let me open in marsh, go floating
after the sawgrass.

FEAR

I. Invisible Thing & Lion

The traps are set, cannons aimed, patient
for you, the chosen target. It wants a trophy

of your glorious head. You have made doctrine
of this war, your belief explains the long winter,

the blight, and names you, its only martyr.
Nothing is there, but you will never believe that.

II. Mosquito & Elephant

Your delicate wires sizzled, dismantled,
it cannot take you whole and lets go.

Left for salvage, you are put back
with solder and epoxy, still alive

but numb in places, your knees twitch,
a buzz remains; you will always taste of lead.

III. Spider & Scorpion

It takes many forms — loosened brick,
a rampant virus, the smashed atom —

and arrives without music. You will try
to seal yourself off with kevlar, duct tape,

and prayer, but your body is so much
soft flesh, between each rib, an open door.

IV. Swallow & Eagle

For altitude, you forsake the low trees,
the easy prey and branches flush with fruit.

The thin air barely sustains you. Sink down
and you could glide as easily as those

beneath you. From the ground, everyone
is smudged and range cannot be measured.

V. Minnow & Leviathan

Your skyscrapers rival mountains, steel peaks
spread and rise upward, the monoliths of cities

calcify. With all your brilliance and strength,
you advance toward the end, lumbering.

You will lose the kingdom, and your successor,
your miniature, will survive you in supple swarms.

EARTHQUAKE

Centuries coupled, as if halves of one, we meant
a constancy of shale, adamantine, and clutched

each other, though our mantle flowed apart.
Our hold splintered and slipped, I tremored

to release you, heaving rivers and boulders,
cracking homes like melons. As Caledonia

and Appalachia were a single range before
a mercy of ocean poured between, so you

and I, riven, will always bear the bands
of silt and shell where once we fit together.

INSOMNIA

We sleep on stilts,
above the floor,

as if the air
in between could change

where we began,
or a cheek against

the ground might
carry us underneath.

PROPERTY

You plus me: the equation of initials equals love.
The wish is cut into bark. Your straight letters

carve clean, but the chisel bites the curve
of mine. I apologize for the alphabet, the triple

odds of eleven in twenty-six. The maple
heart marks this acre of moss our kingdom.

Planting over a bare hill, you tell me
groundcover will need three years to fill in;

you open holes, I press in myrtle roots.
We have time, I answer. I learn the names:

azalea, loosestrife, may apple, and columbine.
You rebuild walls and bound the field, as I bury

bulbs and divide crowns. The ferns have no need
for us, or even each other; they spore

and unfurl alone, as though prehistoric still.
At night, we are bruised from shovel and rake,

too tired to touch. In the quiet, I imagine
the hum is bees building a hive in our walls.

You say the noise is thruway. This house must be
a weapon: sparrows fly into windows, squirrels

die under floorboards, and all the lightbulbs
blow out at once. I wish I understood

the patience of trees in winter, the steadiness
to grow in one place and wait for warmth

to return. But the names of plants are already
a botany of loss. There are snakeskins in the cellar,

little ghostly shifts, but never snakes. I cut holes
in window screens to let out desperate moths.

All spring, I watch for missing tulips; I must
have placed them wrong, with roots reaching up,

and sprouts growing down. I take advice
and retrace my steps. This is where I saw us last,

but we are no longer here, and what remains
is hardpan and all the reasons to be lost.

LITTLE ICE AGE

Confined beyond the timberline, always-winter aches
for green latitudes, for brief reprieve to quarried lakes

relinquished ten millennia past. A shiver to herald
these Siberian years, the cliffs scoured to gravel,

the lettuce smothered in snow. My icebound anchorite,
find your ataraxy in parsnips and arctic hares.

In the cold, your body will renounce its limbs
to keep the heart warm, and spruce will grow dense

in rings. If you survive, plane the wood into violins
which will sing in tones only starvation can teach.

SHIPBROKEN

We said to stay. We said to sail.
She was safer at sea. We were not

safe at sea. Straight out and down.
South by east. South by west.

We thought sea room. We thought
weather. Trusted her. We hoped

like deer. The waves were six feet.
Fifteen feet. Thirty-five. We ran

jacklines. Close-reefed. All hands.
We never stood down. She took on

water. She always did. Planks hissed.
Heavy seas. We were five hundred

miles from the eye. Two hundred
miles. One hundred and thirty-two.

A spar broke. The fore course tore.
We furled. We made fast. We lashed

the helm hard over. We thought
storm-tight. We thought rough days.

Winds were twenty-five knots.
Forty knots. Sixty. She pitched

and listed sharp. We broke ribs
and twisted knees. All of us sick.

None slept. Hove to. Adrift.
We ran the pumps and ran the pumps.

We strained sawdust from the bilge.
We lost prime. The engines stopped.

She flooded. Two feet. Waist deep.
Ten feet. The sole boards floated.

We never said *sinking*. We said
in distress. We mustered on deck.

Waited to abandon ship. *Not yet,*
we said, *still night.* She heeled

starboard. Buried the bow. We said
she's going. We said *don't lose me.*

She rolled on her beam, a tired horse.
Overboard. We fell. We jumped.

Beaten and fouled in her rig.
We swallowed seawater. Swallowed

diesel. We swam clear of her.
Swam to the rafts. We thought

not this. Not her. We were alive.
We drowned. We were never found.

She is fourteen thousand feet down.
Our beds are full of water now.

THREE

NOCTURNAL

I am here again, in the iron-braced dark
where we reassemble ourselves as strangers.
Each of us obedient, drawn below ground,
drowsy as pilgrims.

Recognition here is myopic: I know
only aerosol and exhaustion, shoulder
seams, a port-wine stain, and your secret, still mouth.
Swallowed in tangles,

legs and arms I cannot discern or follow
press me, like the freedom of grass, to let go,
lean in. There is nowhere to fall. I would not
trade this for surface,

but the end comes, sudden as breaking. We leave
our fluorescent privacy, stumble off, gone
mute as plastic horses, unspoiled and blank-eyed,
almost a small tribe.

TORNADO

Spun from the squall line, I am the wrecking ball
of wind you craved, unleashed on this supine plain

where the planet's curve is all that hems horizon,
and you, my only azimuth. Wait for me underground,

a supplicant in the shoveled safety of a root cellar.
You should not see how quick a house is dismantled,

how it will bloom, a peony unfurling wallpaper and tile,
scattering fiberglass and plaster in a bramble of wires:

a history only revealed in ruin. You cannot rebuild
here. Start over and kneel before a new god.

AVIAN

Daylight shrinks, mayflies vanish.
With enough food, geese will forget

to fly south. But not this year.
We lie stiff together, a pair

of matchsticks. I start to tell you
about Arctic Terns, circumpolar

summers, but abandon the end.
We are not so constant.

Outside, the passerines scrape
the air. There is a word

in German for this restlessness
before migration, a word

I cannot pronounce. Willing vagrant,
you are not coming home again.

WILDFIRE

A tree will grow around squirrel bones, enclose
whatever is lost or forgotten: a scythe swung in the trunk,

a hidden tin of panned gold. Up to you, we remain
a knotted stand, every pinecone sealed in resin,

until we petrify in place, but a forest will suffocate
itself, trap the sun and water out. It is no accident

this phosphorus summoned by droughted chaparral,
a pyre to crown the canopy, to burn us both down.

Husband, take your share of buckshot and soot;
forgive me not the fire, but the hesitation to ignite.

VOLCANO

Thirst has made a god of me, and you
my gift, my igneous bride. With goats

milk-dry and wheat hunched in dust,
the village will truss you in lapis beads

and swear you can seduce me into rain.
Without water, the only way to choke

a fire is another fierce enough to steal
its air. Salamandrine, I will return you

obsidian: a sharpened flint to light the fields
ablaze, a knife against their necks, a war.

CONTRITION

A keening culprit, I came unzipped,
unwed. My penance, to be province, to lie

across a millstone bed, ground
to powder, to be wife again. And you,

my conspirator, my paramour, you strapped
your longing to a sail, sent from town,

sent to be lost. But trilobites cluster
beneath your feet on mountaintop

that was once ocean floor and our crime
is a revelation that awaits the murmur of sonar

to be found. Beloved, off the Chalumna River,
a coelacanth was pulled into a fishing boat.

Returned from Cretaceous, returned
ugly and spined, but insisting on itself.

ENDANGERMENT FINDING

Admit our sun is common, a Milky Way twin
to a hundred million more. Even its end

ordinary, no stellar explosion, it will snap
hydrogen to helium then cool to a dense core.

You squint skyward, still wanting the corona
of a bright god, the unconquered sun that chose us

to spin around. But there is no need for tributes
of maize and falcon wings while we burn

the oil of light left eons ago. You may ratify
the droughts and downpours, assign blame

for melting ice and rising seas, but I can count
more kinds of hammers than turtles;

we need instinct, not law. The dogs of Pompeii
howled for days, even snakes slithered

from Helice. In the Gallatin Range, the bears
left the forest. At night, a slice of mountain shook

down, sleepers drowned in their beds, soaked
in waves off the lake. When the ground stilled,

the bears returned covered with mud. Hush.
Listen to our internal combustion rumble.

There is more elegance in turning photon
to electron to motion. Let us trade the old sun

for the new one, sustain ourselves, wet and green,
within this delicate spindle of axis and orbit.

SWARM

A gathered swoon above a sweet expanse,
I am a darkling flush, a pollen-heady

descent upon your lustrous acres. My hunger
sings the stridulant percussion of limbs.

Be still, as I devour every stem
and leaf, swallow you, husk, spikelet

and seed, ravish down to root, until
we are enfolded, a fuse of verdant instar.

From the exhausted moan of damp earth,
my scion, we molt together, engulf a jungle.

MIGRATION

Armored with a netting of tires, the barge crawls,
sets a path of moorings along the harbor.
Summer anchors sink in the silt, their white floats
bowing to current,

waiting. I am tethered here, while you chart home,
north through narrow clemency, spared between sharp
Carolina coast and Atlantic beaten
barrier islands.

ICELAND

Once a forest was here: call it legend.
The first arrival in dayless winter, the timbers
felled for pastures or burned. What remained

was hewn for boats when the sun returned
in excess, as if wished for too hard.
A thousand years without trees has winnowed

this island, left us little but ice. The sheep
stagger over crumbled lava fields,
a plate of potatoes and salt cod is enough.

You say there were never birch, insist on red
in rhyolite, but refuse the lupine, foreign
and unplanned, though it clutches

scree nothing else can hold. Sometimes
even love is invasive; let it turn
pumice to soil, bring us back to green.

NATURAL HISTORY

For Faro

To say love is why explorers trekked north
with oilskin and sextants believing mastodons
were still alive is fiction, but I would haul a sled

over tundra, hoping a herd survived, hoping you
will survive. My body opens like an umbrella
as you become an abstract of history, speeding

through evolution until you are covered
with arboreal fur. Before you have fingerprints,
or even hands, your ribs unfurl in fiddleheads.

They articulate in pairs. The world without us
is nameless. There are words for all the molten ages
before the seabed bloomed, but none for after us,

not even in Latin. Our imagination spurns
extinction, even when shown a dinosaur egg
or skies once darkened by pigeons. In the museum,

a diorama waits for the future, a camouflage
of blankness. I surrender to your small chance
of being, though you are only a faint shadow

in sonar, a muffled thrum. This love is talons
and wild valor against the baying of hounds.
Glass boxes bear sabertooth skulls, meteorites,

and tracks in volcanic ash. The revolutions
are numerous. A blue whale drifts from the ceiling,
navel wide as a dinner plate, a half-ton heart

on the floor underneath. It is doubtful hearts
will be larger in the future. I want to promise you
permanence, my constant orbit, but even continents

are revisions. I am only your diving bell in water
hemmed by shifting plates. For now, the only name
I give you is my own, though maps are drawn

for seas ten million years ahead. In Ethiopia,
a rift will open wide enough for water
to pour a new coastline and drown the valley

where the skeleton of a woman, not quite human
or ape, was found. As you take my bones
for your own, my greedy passenger, the certainty

of elements is all I have. Your inheritance
of calcium was starfish, then mountain,
then lettuce, and will be a third of what remains

when we are afterward and underwater again.
Bones will say stop before they snap. To reach
the heart, a surgeon cranks open the awning

of ribs until they gasp. My chest expands
without lathe or scalpel, only the force
of your arrival loosening the baleen corset.

To say I made you is inaccurate. You make
yourself from secret blueprints, a shapeling
clutching a manifest of your demands, the parts

salvaged from my body. The revolutions are sudden.
In-between marine, you command dark tides
and destroy me in your making. You wind

umbilical inside, as if to stay. I let the doctors
carve me open like cardboard. My body
could have been a grave. After nothing familiar,

all you know is survival, a green bank of yelping.
You practice a pantomime of instinct, crying
in my accent, grasping for branches with flung-out

arms, and rooting for my breast. Intricacies
of milk and sleep dismantle me. I empty
myself into you, hollowing by the ounce.

There are seven white rhinos when you are born.
A year later, six. I try to tally the animals
vanished in my lifetime and lose count. The frogs

in Costa Rica are gone, an ibex of the Pyrenees,
clouded leopards in Taiwan, the Caspian tiger
and Java tiger, a boa in Mauritius, and grizzly bears

last seen beside the headwaters of the Yaqui River.
Their names chant a grim litany for you to learn,
a half-formed loss. We are in a great dying.

You are going to die. No longer my throat
or temple, the most breakable part of my body
is on the outside now. A javelin anchors the air

between us. Fifty billion creatures have lived
among antlered legends and trampled mud,
but only one percent still ambles leeward.

Dream wary, I feign courage or madness.
There may be no refuge in greenwood,
but you are a stockade of light. I abide

in your clear voice in the grass. You have
only words for what you love: apple,
book, and home. You name the rest yourself:

cat a plaintive moan, spiders are wriggling
fingers, the sky is hands waved above.
But you have no word for me. The question

of who I am confounds you, as though asked
to name a reflection. Not mother or son: *us*.
We are a coral reef, a pod of whales, descendants

of slime, an endless expanding. Under the city,
aquifer fills with seawater, slowly drawing
the avenues down. Someday, someone

will find our ribs in a midden of oyster shells,
ship hulls, and wooden doors. Instead of a cage,
may they lash our bones together as a raft.

NOMAD

In a time of faint beasts, no room
is left in the boats. With thin hands,

we huddle sheep and dip a hundred
reeds in mud. The nets wheel away

so often now, sinking though days
poured furious over threshing feet.

As though dared in a foreign tongue
to knot our sleeves, we swim through

broken oars, shout off slender days.
Snakes may cling to trees, and men

tear at bread, but the sky stays hinged.
Only heaven is full of furniture.

We harness ourselves over and over,
wherever hope is a yellow shore.

NOTES

"Disturbance"
Paraphrases Immanuel Kant's writings on the sublime in *Critique of Judgment*.

"White Matter"
Uses language taken from the grand jury in Ferguson, MO in 2014 which failed to indict Police Officer Darren Wilson for the death of Michael Brown, an unarmed African-American teenager.

"Middle Flight"
Quotes balloonists Joseph-Michel Montgolfier, Jacques Charles, and Colonel Joseph Kittinger. Refers to the early aeronauts Sophie Blanchard and John Wise, and cluster balloonists Larry Walters, Adelir Antonio de Carli, and Jonathan R. Trappe.

"Reptilian"
Inspired by the painting "Self-Portrait as Swamp Queen II" by Julie Heffernan.

"Shipbroken"
Draws on first-hand accounts of the sinking of the Tall Ship Bounty on October 29, 2012 off the coast of North Carolina during Hurricane Sandy.

"Natural History"
Adapts quotes from Georges Cuvier's "A Discourse on the Revolutions on the Surface of the Globe."

ABOUT THE AUTHOR

Robin Beth Schaer was raised in New York. She was educated at Colgate University and Columbia University. She has received fellowships from Yaddo, Djerassi Resident Artists Program, Saltonstall Foundation, and Virginia Center for the Creative Arts. She teaches writing in New York City, and worked as a deckhand aboard the Tall Ship Bounty, a 180-foot full-rigged ship lost in Hurricane Sandy. She lives in Brooklyn, NY with her husband, the fiction writer Anthony Tognazzini, and their son, Faro.